ISBN: 978-1-300-01608-3

Edited, formatted and published by
Vincent Hayley
vhayley@aol.com

Hayley Word Graphics

TO MY MOTHER,

from whom I learned sensitivity to art, and

TO MY FATHER,

from whom I learned sensitivity to people

Odysseys: The Poet in Us All

Table of Contents

Indexes

INTRODUCTION

Creativity is an attribute that we often think *other* people have. We applaud it in artists, choreographers, composers, writers, and others, but seem to ignore or downplay it in ourselves. That we do is in some ways a tragedy. Creativity adds a dynamism and an enjoyment to life — a vitality that can be ours without a lot of effort. It may indeed be more readily available the less we force it.

EVOLUTION: ME, A POET?

As a youngster I was sad at observing that my mother had talent which she and others seemed not to acknowledge or not to appreciate much. The family library contained notebooks of poetry she wrote as a high-school student. I wondered why didn't she publish it, why didn't she share her talent. It seemed to me that on that shelf, beauty was collecting dust.

I enjoyed reading her poetry — and sometimes the poetry of others. Edgar Allan Poe's poems had rhyme, rhythm, and feeling that echoed in me as I read them. Edna St. Vincent Millay's "World, world, I cannot hold thee close enough" expressed such joy, and Robert Frost's "Two roads diverged . . . and I – I took the one less traveled by, And that has made all the difference" was a declaration with which I identified. I did not like a lot of poetry; poems often seemed cumbersomely worded or unintelligible, or to express melancholy. But for me there were some poems that were alive.

Usually the poems I read were in books, and written by well-known writers. That, I imagine, fostered in me the notion that literary talent was rare. Then I saw a television program that revealed that might not be so. It was a "Camera 3" show that featured Kenneth Koch teaching poetry writing to young everyday students in a public elementary school in New York City. The poems they werewriting were sensitive, graphic, imaginative expressions of their world. Koch encouraged those youngsters, and what those youngsters revealed was that they too, as young as they were, and as nameless to me as the numbers on their school buildings, were creative — and were enjoying their creativity!

Later I picked up a copy of Koch's *Wishes, Lies, and Dreams* in which many of the poems of those same youngsters appear. As I read, I thought what fun to let imagination ramble, to create imaginary worlds of wishes into words, to manufacture jolly lies, knowing they are lies and yet enjoying them, opening ourselves to dreams that are simultaneously fantasy and real, that are vivid and colorful and part of our lives. What these youngsters produced was not only psychological insight and release, but powerful, beautiful visions of emotions and experiences and perspectives that are within us all. What frequently resulted was literary art.

As months and years ticked by, I discovered other books by Koch. *Rose, Where Did You Get That Red?* is a collection of poems by elementary, junior high, and high school students whom he had taught. That book has a different format than *Wishes, Lies, and Dreams* and seems less fluid than the first book. Yet, in *Rose* are writings of young, sensitive, imaginative, creative individuals.

Koch's *I Never Told Anybody* is a compilation of poems of retired people whom he taught at their residence, a nursing home. As with his younger students, he focused on themes of color and sound and touch and dreams, etc. With the retired folks he seemed to highlight another feature, memory. The poems that these older writers created are more than nostalgia; they are accounts of human relationships, relationships of feeling and humanity.

The more these older people produced poems, the more sensitive and artistic their poems were, in style, beauty, and impact. The structure of their poems did not appear tobe forced, but to flow from their own gradually accumulating comfort with poetry — their poetry. Again, everyday people were creating literary beauty.

In *I Never Told Anybody* Koch attempts to analyze his experience as a poetry teacher — which methods of teaching seemed to work better than others, and why — which themes seemed more productive than others, and why. I studied Koch's remarks, made notes about them, and compared his thinking with my own impressions of his teaching and the poetry that came out of his teaching.

I had been a teacher myself, a college instructor of psychology, was familiar with styles and philosophies of teaching, and sometimes felt pleased and often felt frustrated with my own efforts at teaching.

I was unemployed in 1977. I enrolled in a job-skills development program of the federal Comprehensive Employment and Training Act (CETA). My title: environment resource person. I was learning skills to be an environmental educator. The program site was the

Elbanobscot Environmental Center in Sudbury, Massachusetts. Those of us in Elbanobscot CETA were offered an opportunity to teach mini courses to each other.

I got brave, and decided to try to teach poetry writing. I wanted to free myself from my previous rigid methods of teaching, and to experiment with some of the methods Koch had used.

To my surprise and delight, my Elbanobscot class spontaneously and literally applauded at the end of my first session. I was aware that they were not only applauding me, but maybe also applauding themselves, their own creativity that they were perhaps beginning to discover anew.

I tried my hand at teaching poetry writing to a group of fifth graders too — at a public school. I was told later that the regular teacher of those youngsters saw I was succeeding when one of her students who did not write before was writing during my class. I was a guest teacher and was with that class for only an hour.

In that class as with the older Elbanobscot group, I ignored problems of writing, did not comment on grammar or spelling or say when I thought a student had misunderstood the literary style or theme I had in mind. Instead I emphasized what I liked about their writings — and there was much to like.

Elbanobscot had a second CETA group of unemployed adults later, in 1978. I was a guest teacher for them for one session, four hours, one day. Again, quality poetry was a result!

METHODS OF TEACHING

The methods that I used often then, and use now, are relatively easy. I usually begin with a few introductory remarks about creativity and the enjoyment we can have in opening ourselves to our own creativity. I talk about Koch and the pleasures I've had reading his books.

I then try to focus on a particular kind of poem or poetry theme — poems in which fantasy is emphasized, or comparison, or sound, or color, or so on. I read aloud some examples, often poems from Koch's books, poems written by his students. Usually they are happy poems.

I do not stress form; I stress feeling — the feelings that I have from these poems. I read a poem aloud once, and then read it again, aloud, slower than before, commenting about its imagery, or whatever, as I read along. I might useone poem or more than one, or parts of poems.

I invite members of the class to write a similar poem. Sometimes I attempt to help a group of writers loosen upby asking them to write a fantasy poem as the first exercise. Before they write fantasy, I share some fantasy poems aloud.

I encourage students not to concentrate on making sense — instead to write quickly, to let the pen or pencil almost write by itself, not to think much about what they write,but just write. I might give them a first line, and have themwrite whatever other lines seem to come to their minds.

An invitation to a unique mixture of senses can be a catalyst to creativity. Once in a while I propose to writers that with eyes closed they touch an object and imaginewhat color it is, and what has a similar color. Or I might suggest that an unlabeled scent be smelled with eyes closed — what texture is thought of? How does it feel without actually touching it? What scenes are recalled or imagined?

After we have written some poems, either I have each writer read aloud to the class, that is, share with the class, his or her poem, or I collect the poems and I read them aloud to the class without mentioning the name of the writer. As I read I comment about what I like. If the writeris the one doing the reading, I make notes about what I like – imagery or phrases, and so on — and then after the poem has been read once, I offer my positive remarks. After a poem has been read once and I, or I and other members of the class, have commented, I often like to have the poem read aloud once again.

A group poem, one written by more than one person, is to some extent improvisational when it is first read to a class. For a group poem, I ask students to write a few lines either on a particular subject such as my sweater, or on a general theme. With a theme poem I might provide a line or two to stimulate imagination. Afterward, I gather lines and read them aloud in random order, reading them together as one long poem, and might sometimes repeat the first lines I gave as a method of unifying the poem while I read. Later, when I edit a group poem for publication I usually rearrange the order of the lines and make form changes for continuity.

A follow-up procedure, that takes much time, is that after a class I collect not only group poems but individual poems, edit them, type and reproduce them. I distribute copies of the entire class collection to each member of the class.

THIS COLLECTION

Some of the people from the first and second CETA groups and I got together with other friends to write more. It was an opportunity for us to develop our literary skills and to share our enjoyment of both creativity and poetry. This book is mostly a selection from our works. A dozen or so other poems in this collection are by other friends of mine who have not been in our group.

Those of us who periodically met for poetry allowed ourselves the fun of writing. Sometimes what we said does not seem to make practical sense. As in the poetry classes I taught, we intentionally let that happen. Spontaneity has been an asset. In a real sense, creativity is enhanced by being open and receptive to our own subconscious. Conscious thinking can at the beginning be an obstacle, as Koch observed. It has been my experience that letting ideas out, putting them on paper before thinking about them, and then later reviewing and perhaps refining orrewording them, is a more productive approach than placing them from the onset in a straightjacket of customary reason.

At the back of this book are indexes where our works are grouped according to subject and with a focus on method. Some poems were submitted without the writer's name appearing. Those writers are identified as anonymous. Our techniques — becoming a tree or sunlight, putting senses together in new combinations, attention on color, and so on — were used as ways of seeing the world afresh and of sparking our imaginations. Through your reading, you might come up with literary innovations of your own.

Most of the poems in this book were written while we were with each other. We wrote together, and read aloud to each other what we had written. We shared with each other not for criticism but for mutual enjoyment. I later edited, arranging where lines break and deciding on what punctuation and form to use. The words, ideas, and flow of expression are those of the individual writers.

What we have written is poetry, literature both creative and rich.

Vincent Hayley

A CONFUSION OF SENSES

Isolated like a moon
Emotion turns inward, I.
A tumbling of creators
Sounding like a scoop of
        I screams.
Why don't I join a bark of dogs;
At least then I belong.

Wim Jansen

A dog.
What a friend, all tongue and ears,
Lively, jumping, friendly, loving,
Seeking, beseeching,
Wanting a loving hand to caress,
Scratch his ears,
Talk to him.
His is a loyalty that knows no bounds.
A protector.
The not so silent sentry.

Sheila Scheufele

ADVICE TO THE BEGINNING POET . . .

Winged rings obsess the spider's home;
Top bats circle the wool domes
        of hats
        like that --
And woo the sun to rise.

Rose petals curl out of green,
And hide the leaves now rarely seen
        at dawn
        and yawn
Like guys who think they're wise.

So heap your poems like seeds –
But do watch out for weeds
        upon this heap
        of paper -- but keep
The good ones home for cries and sighs.

Rosie Rosenzweig

AFTER

Clothespins sit, bluejays
        on an empty clothesline.
Trees spin spiderweb shadows
        on the white, still sea of snow.
Dogs bark in distant lands.
A lively little winged friend
        flutters across space.

A quiet tiger leaps
        like the sound of a falling rose petal
        onto a sunbathed sill.
The furnace chugs
        as if deep within a merchant ship.
Black Cat and Fred sit purring like doves
        on the sunsea table behind me.

Birds chatter and scatter.
A few snowdrops fall
        from their roofbed.
Roelof mutters, then barks
        at the stageplay she watches
        from her front-row-center seat
        no ticket required.
The sun is awake and happy.

Vincent Hayley

AND OH SO BEAUTIFUL

Moving about; almost dancing
Together, but yet alone.
Full of color . . . harmonious.
So small as one,
But together their strength is unmatched.

Anonymous

A passle of petals floated by,
A shower of softness from the sky;
Floating and flying, airy and light,
Some from the left and some from the right.
No sound is made as they tiptoe down
To lay themselves silently on the ground.
A carpet of color they now make.
Oriental? Or a myriad lake?

Sheila Scheufele

A pencil is part of a tree
That never realized
It had writing capabilities.

Charlotte Cardeiro

A PICTURE OF POEMS

I long to paint with words
The landscape in my mind,
Stroking on verbs of birds in flight,
Splashing the noun of dawn's daylight.
It's really a canvas on which I build,
A picture of poems, dreams yet fulfilled.

Jane Plasse

APRIL DAYS

Come with me
to a land of buzz and fuzz
Where apples dream
and dogs build nests of love,
Where water cries
and shadows smile and play,
Where ears hear yellow
and fingers soothe the sky,
Where saltair chats with lions' teeth
and chipmunks taste the sun.
Let's bathe ourselves in dreams
where trees dance
and fields shout happy notes.
I *am* the sun.

Vincent Hayley

ARMS

I know these pine trees well
I am mother to them.
They now stand guardian to me.
The sturdy arms have held me
        and my children,
Nurtured us
Through many storms,
And I have loved them
And nurtured them too.
Many a winged friend has shared its haven.
Home, haven, refuge for us all.

Bobby Robinson

ARTIST OF THE SEASON

The wind is orange
In the morning sun.
A peacock of autumn.

Vincent Hayley

AS I WATCH AND LISTEN

Ripples.
Twitters.
A distant vehicle –
And a tractor whirring.

Leaves scratching.
Feathers whistling.
Caw, caw, caw.
Arf, arf. Arf, arf, arf.

A far-off metal bird, humming.
Human voices.
A housedoor closing.

Wings flapping in a pond.
A slow stream over a dam.
Ducks vocalizing.

A page of paper flapping.
Dried seeds floating.

An insect stroking.
A thrown breeze pimpling the waters.

Vincent Hayley

AWAKENING

Bubbles of the damp night
          glisten on the dawn grass.
The smell of melon
          rides the morning air.
Whistles emanate slowly
          out of sunlit trees.
Green blades of time dance
          slow-motion dances.
Morning is here.

Vincent Hayley

A warm smile as I enter this circle
    to land on the runway
    from the nose to the rose
    ah!
I can't seem to leave the fire now
    for I am within it,
    and it is within me –
Happy, snappy, leaping, dancing, warm –
    ah so warm!
    free flowing,
    consuming the wood,
    leaving ashes
    with which to build another day.

Charlotte Cardeiro

BACK IN THE SADDLE AGAIN

Those good ole westerns;
Sitting in front of the TV,
John Wayne and his sauntering walk –
They don't make them like they used to:
The Big Valley,
Gunsmoke,
Bonanza –
An era gone yet continuously rerun
'Til you know every script by heart.
Riding out with the boys,
Jumping on your horse,
Setting out to head them off at the pass.
Gone. Yet when I hear such music
It's as though nothing has changed
Back in my youth,
And I've just come in off the range.

Jane Plasse

Birches,
My favorite tree,
As it probably was Frost's,

Why is it my favorite,
Because it stands out
Amongst the others?
Or maybe, the big old birch
Outside of Grandpa's farm.
Away from city pavement
And nesting in its arches I feel good.

Birches,
My favorite tree.

Anonymous

Blue, yellow, brown, gray, tan
Light, dark, red, these are
Some of the colors in
The world of the trees, the
Sky the ground the people.
No order of the eye to
See because this is the
World I see but now
I'm blind
And now I can really see.

Anonymous

Bower of birch – white against the gloom
Bower of birch – tormented, twisted
Bower of birch reaching to the sky
Waiting, peaceful

Bower of birch – concealing life
Bower of birch – birds sing within
Bower of birch – leafless, majestic
Spring returns

Anonymous

BROCHURE

A new encyclopedia!
How to do this and how to work that.
Gadgets and inventions, hydrofoil,
Space ships, scientific principles!
The logic behind Xeroxing,
Snake oil for the new space age.
These things were made for you and me.
Who was it now that made that tree?

Rosie Rosenzweig

Caw – Caw. Mee 0 Maw
Kee . . . Kee   hi diddle di de
Twew-twew twew   How do you chew?
Di di di di di – . . . a serendipity.

Barry Marchette

CETA PILGRIMS

Polonius: "What do you read, my lord?"
Hamlet: "Words, words, words."
Shakespeare's Hamlet, Act II, Scene II

A metaphor of poets,
we sit unwinding our skein of heads
Into a wealth of words,
a moment of philosophies, a hill of creeds.
We pile and pile our dreams
into a loft of papers, bursting a rift of seams.
The only line that made sense
was a ragged run, not worth a damn of pence,
A carving of similes, cut into an old whorl,
a circle of images, a pull of whirlpools,
But it seeds a blossom of bulbs.

Rosie Rosenzweig

CLARE DE LUNE

Love is dripping from your guitar,
Running, softly flowing all over me,
Framing me to its own harmony.
I surrender my hurry to the strings
Through which your love flows.

Charlotte Cardeiro

Come with me to a land of love
Where ears hear yellow
And fingers soothe the sky,
Where weasels rule the world
And puppies never cry,

Where I exist in peace with the land I love,
Where things are just so mellow
And linger just so high,

Where time goes backward,
Poems don't rhyme,
And we'll feel good
All the time.

The wine is bright purple
And the moon never touches the sky,
But the boy always asks why.

There you will meet Jungle Jane.
On a tree she swings
And a song she sings,
And the song she sings
For Tarzan to attract
And the same way to react,
To swing to the highest tree.
There you will see
With her fingers they will
Soothe the sky.

Why?

Come with me to a land of love
Where doves are doves
And swim in purple seas
And smell the pinky dew dust
Through their ears.

Anonymous

Perch upon a pinnacle mind
Of green meadow mornings
And a delicate daisy daze,
Where eyes see sunshine
And rainbows fill the heart,

Where the birds fly, the hawk, the raven, the dove
Where heaven meets the earth,
Where life moves faster than eye,

Where the nose smells clouds
As they float gently by,
And the ears are tickled by the stars
Falling down from above.

Jump this abyss of sanity
With senses ringing to spear reality
Softly speaking.

Come with me to a land of love
Where minds meet minds
Beneath the billowy softness of the clouds.
Come, come – touch the sky with me.

And as you reach out
The clouds are marshmellows
And lightning is the fire
And we sit and roast the clouds.

A group poem from lines submitted by
members of an Elbanobscot/CETA mini course,
SENSITIVITY THROUGH POETRY WRITING,
April 11th, 1978

COMPANION

Of all my friends this summer day
My favorite is nearby I say.

It waves to me while I am ill
That giant tree outside my sill.

A thousand hands of purple brown
Flutter there with gentle sound.

Vincent Hayley

DAYDREAM

The airplane lazily buzzing in a faraway fair sky
        on a summer afternoon.
The screech of the drawer filled with bubble-gum funnies
        in a chest my mother owned as a child.
The softness of the quilt Nana Taylor made before I was born.

I am supposed to be napping.
I am naughty.
I hate naps!

Marilyn Komins

DAY OF DIAMONDS, DAY OF LIGHT

The icicle is a slow-motion tear.
It is a diamond in the sky.
It is a crystal tree hanging upside down,
A roofgate effervescent in the sun,
A cane for strolling purple gnomes.
It is a frozen probe into silent space,
A radiant bracelet made by time.

Vincent Hayley

DREAMS

Where do shadows go at night?
They dance with the curious moonbeams
        on the floor.
They try to bake the naked lasagna,
        to feed the ferocious tiger.
They ride with Motorcycle Mongrel
        to the edge of sea dreams
        only to find the wrinkles on the ocean
        speaking of days when shadows made us aware
        of light,
        life,
        love,
And music was their habitat.

Wim Jansen

ESMERELDA'S PLEA

Waste not flowers upon my grave –
These are for the living.
I cannot see or touch or smell;
If flowers you offer, you can go to hell!
Your love and prayers will nicely suffice my dear
If, of course, they are sincere.
Flowers are for the living to save.
Lay your love upon my grave.

Charlotte Cardeiro

EVEN ' DAWN

In a village of leaves
        along the reservoir shore
Strolls the poet with his thoughts.

Miniature alps roll along
        the gray-blue sea
With the breeze of dusk.

Waterpimples move upon the water
        like a thrown fishernet.
Leafboats, as if moored, bob on the surface.

An ant climbs upon the poet's wrist
        watching as he writes,
While the sun shines yellow-white.

Vincent Hayley

EVERYTIME

Every time I feel too sad and lonely
Every time the blues come down my way
I close my eyes and dream that we're together
Like two clouds that are drifting through the day
Their own way

Every time I feel I cannot go on
Every time I think the end is near
I think of you and then I feel the sunshine
And that just seems to take those blues away
Far away

For it's your love that brings me joy
And takes away the pain
Just like a rainbow paints the sky
Right after it has rained
The gentle way you call my name
Can soothe the roughest day
And it's your love I'll always need
And by your side I'll stay
Stay

Every time the world just seems to close in
I don't want to wait and see things through
I call your name and then I feel surrounded
By feelings that are meaningful and true
I love you

Every time I feel too sad and lonely
Every time the blues come down my way
I close my eyes and dream that we're together
Like two clouds that are drifting through the day
Their own way

Jerry DePinto

EXCITING RINGLE-POO

Oh swerzy, here comes the Ramadoozle !
Po and Mup, you stay here
And wait for the lock-a-poo.
Po, will you pick up Ring-a-ping and Swirzy?
We'll all meet at the dersh.
Zeel Isn't this fun!

Charlotte Cardeiro

EXPERIENCES IN THE LIFE OF A TOOTHBRUSH
or Teeth That I Have Known in the Dark and Scary Cavern
Drowning in that Paste of Foam

The nightmares I have had in there
        while scrubbing up and down,
        up and down,
        down and up.
        'round and 'round
        (just let me out!)
Then you rinse me in that water of ice
        smile in a mirror and think how nice,
When it's me who's done the work myself
        only to be put back on the shelf.
I think a statue should be made of me
        for all the teeth that I have raised!

Jane Plasse

EXPLORATIONS

An undulating ladder of white, yellow, and black
The caterpillar like roaming radar
Swiveled across the giant leaf,
Climbed to a green ridge,
Then over to a side;
Probed into space,
And moved on.

Vincent Hayley

FANTAMETER

Finolatum is not abatum
But absecuvio is surely realio
Whoopsiehoopsie was feeling groopsie
Because cateconia caught ammonia
And googalophigus lost the omnibus
But mousearonica was a gonica
Honestly where does that leave me?

Sheila Scheufele

FESTIVAL

This season of fall
Is a garden in a tree
Rich with squash yellow
And tomato red.
The green peapods
Lace through the muted pinks
And subtle rusts
Of Spanish onion.
It is a feast
Tasted by the eye.

Vincent Hayley

FIFTH-GRADE VISIONS

Vince's sweater is like a furry kitten
    and is as red as a tomato.
Vince's sweater is the color of warm rushing lava.
    It feels like a shaved sheep.
Vince's sweater is as red as an eraser.
    It is a dull red, like a movie star's racer.
    It feels as soft as a kitten
    and as scratchy like one too.
    My kitten loves me
    but the sweater is red as someone's mad face.
Vince's shirt is as red as vampire blood,
    as furry as a pineapple.

Vince's sweater is like the color of a crayon.
Vince's sweater feels like a piece of itchy yarn.
The sweater is like a warm blanket
    and as red as an apple.
Vince's sweater is like the trees during fall.
Vince's sweater feels like the chalk on the chalkboard.
Vince's sweater is like a color of a rug.
Vince's sweater is the color of a barn swallow.
Vince's sweater is like a big red grape
    and as furry as a thorn bush.

Vince's sweater is like a big maroon leaf.
Vince's sweater is as rough as an unsanded piece of wood.
Vince's sweater is like wool.
Vince's sweater is like a "colorful sweater".
Vince's sweater is like a flower in bloom.
Vince's sweater is like someone is making everybody laugh.
Vince's sweater is as red as a dark red crayon.
It's as fuzzy as a rug.

Vince's sweater is soft and furry
like a lamb with colored fur.
It is purple like grapes on a vine.
Vince's sweater is as dark as night
and is big like my desk.
Vince's sweater is like the color of a leaf in the fall.
Vince's sweater looks like a shirt and a big maroon ball.
It feels soft.
It has a different color in it and looks like red
and is like a cat's fur.
Vince's sweater is like a blackout when it's raining
a dark rose in the summer.

A group poem from lines by
Mrs. Paulson's 5th grade,
Claypit Hill School,
Wayland, Massachusetts
October 13th, 1977

Fingers, fingers, fingers
Reaching, grasping, climbing, stretching
Out, out, out, east, west, north, south
Looking up, reaching out, stretching
Climbing--
Pushing up, up, up;
Grey and green and brown
And red softly surround
Me in my darkness
(And yet I remain distinct),
Softly branching out, ever
So quiet upon the
Shining surface of
My face, tickling
Me forever with
Its softness.

Anonymous

FIRESIDE FLOWERS

The roses are like my hopes and dreams for the future
        opening full and wide.
They are as soft as down,
        as sweet as spring,
        and as red as your face by the fire.
To touch them makes me warm
        and feel you deep in me.
I hold these flowers of red velvet
        even with the thorns they hide,
And I hold you.

Jane Plasse

FRIEND

Poetry,
You open me up
To another world
Inside.

A world of color
And life,
A world of new touch
And sights,

Of grasshoppers yelling
And moonbeams dreaming,
Of minds entwining
And saltshakers crying,

Where time is rearranged
And size is not proclaimed
A measure
But a thoughtframe.

Come, poetry –
Vivid, alive, bathing –
Invite my dreams to flow
In kaleidoscope phrase,

To look with ears
And listen with eyes,
To paint with words
My smiles and sighs.

Vincent Hayley

GLASSES OF IMAGINATION

Books like seeds planted on the carpet
Waiting to green the landscape of my mind;
Books, like a house protecting the contents
From the unready, unreading.
Books, like a rabbit run in the open field;
I can peek and imagine the views it encloses.
Books, standing on edge, showing their faces,
Asking to be understood.
Books, scattered like ideas,
Waiting to open and build whatever one wishes.
Book, door, window, manhole, entrance,
Glasses of my imagination.

Wim Jansen

gray passivity –
indecision,
blandness,
a waiting.

achromatic,
nonacrobatic,
not even monochromatic.

value is what artists name it –
a proper term,

for its meaning is time to rest,
letting things ride,
an unthink,
a pause

between appearance of color
at beginning
and end.

Marilyn Komins

HARMONY

The fire rises up in warmth –
        home, feeling good.
My mind will glow and glow with rays of flames
        into the harmony
        only my fire transforms things into.

Wim Jansen

HAY!

Swish – splish – to and fro
Tanish and yellowish – see it grow
All summer long from green to brown
Until the fall – it's all cut down

Corinne Nichols

Hea Ia goa
Humu Humu nuku nuku
Apu a-a
Redredia Redfredia
No accrudgeon
Udgeons
Allowed at 2
Booooo –

Kathy Cardeiro

Here in Camden
The many sailboats float in the quiet blue harbor.
On the arch of green, visitors sit and watch
As the afternoon mellows.
A yellow frisbee sails silently.
Lovers lie by the water
And walk by the shores of time
In this September land.

Vincent Hayley

He stood there, naked and trim,
Not ashamed of his smooth and shapely body.
The wind caressed him
          like a warm cloak.

He was at peace with himself
But afraid of others,
Afraid of admirers.

Off he dashed across the soft sand
          and dove into the blue-gray bay,
Not so much in fear as in joy,
Splashing in the waters of refreshment.

Vincent Hayley

Hi there –
Enjoying the day --
Thanks for not blowing smoke
At me that way.
I know sometimes I am wet and cold
And blustery and windy and very bold.
But now and again I can be
Warm and friendly as sweet as thee.

Hi there – yes, you,
Playing in my being.
Thanks for coming. Thanks
For the singing.

Anonymous

HOUSE

People come and go – sun comes – night comes,
But there is a time when I feel
Rested – sundown to sunset –
The quietness and solitude I like.
It gets cold, but when people come
I get warm.

I feel some people are welcome and
Some are not.
The people that are welcome treat me
With respect --
The unwelcome ones treat me
With disrespect.

My house is for people to visit.
If they did not I would be lonely
And miss them.

Mary Loftus

I am a tree.
Not only a tree, but an oak tree
And a strong one.
Many a country has chosen
My image
As an image of strength and beauty.

I am standing on top of a hill.
I did not have it easy.
I had to endure the storm, the cold, the ice,
The snow, the rain, the sun,
Rabbits, the wild deer, the people.

That's why I am strong.
I am 500 years old.
I have seen many a thing
And could tell you many stories,
About the big forest which once surrounded me,
It's long gone –
The Shawmut Indians having their smoke signals
Next to me.
The Puritans –
The troops of George Washington.

Now I am protected by an environmental education center
And youngsters of 1978 are admiring me.

I hope they watch me very carefully
And protect me
Against the termites and ants,
Those who kill slowly but surely
From the inside out.

With this assurance
I will still be another 500 years around
And that will make me 1000 –
Wonder how things will look then –

Anonymous

I am the hill, rain
Beaten and pummeled
By the winds,
Deposited harshly
By the icy rage of eons ago.
I've lost some form,
No longer peaked,
But squat and rounded down beneath.
Mother Mountain
Calls from above
Reminding me how I was.

Anonymous

I am the squirrel
so hungry at this
colden day,
My food is dwindled down,
the nuts are chewed away,
The spring, so long in coming
leaves my belly bare,
And I keep on thinking
I'm soon to be thin air.
How am I like a squirrel?
I never used to care;
And now with my tummy empty,
my identity left someplace,
My little tiny feet
trying so hard to erase
the tracks across the tree limbs
into my new home,
All I seem to think about
is that high interest loan.
I guess I can't live long this way
over my head in money
and always without bread;
It's time to return to nature,
to be a squirrel in my natural head.

Anonymous

IMAGES OF ICICLES

Icicles – long sparkling mirrors,
Glistening stalactites from heaven,
Solid drops of dew
Lengthening and changing by day,
Becoming rigid by night,
Frozen in a pattern of jagged teeth,
Gripping and clenching until sun returns,
Then releasing in shining tears.

Bobby Robinson

I'm swaying with my arms entwined
with my friends
My feet are cool and covered
with leaves
The wind is blowing us back and forth
back and forth
The squirrels tickle as they climb up
my side
I hear the birds' songs as they rest
on me
All the while the wind is blowing us
back and forth
back and forth

Tally Groves

IN FLIGHT WITH A BLIND BIRD

Soaring I go,
The cool of noontime on my face
Into a land of snowwhite blue.

Vincent Hayley

In the green yard full of green trees
Sits a green chair
Where I sit with my green pen and green paper
And watch green birds fly through green skies.

A green frog leaps through green minutes
From green water, and explores a green world.

Green apples hang gently from
Green branches
And sway in a green breeze
In the warm green sun.

Vincent Hayley

In the library, the mice read quietly.
Squeak go their long tails across the shining pages
As they run from word to word.
The librarian looks up silently,
Wondering who is making the
Small squeeeeeeeeaks.
A flat page flaps
Like a sail in the wind
Or thunder far away;
But there is no rain, and the blue sky is bright,
And the books are being read.

Vincent Hayley

I pad down the mountain,
It's Berry Creek Path.
With willow on my back
I wander and meander;
There's no hurrying here.
You can hear the river rushing –
        though it's a mile away
        smileaway.
I really don't want to arrive,
Just hear the river symphony
Rushing, singing up the mountain,
Filling up the trees –

Kathy Cardeiro

I see you, friends
        Standing proud,
Reaching out,
        To touch the cloud.
I see wind caress,
        Cool rain soothe,
While you so gently,
        Gently move.
I see your Halloween costumes bright
        Which too soon
        You drop from sight;
You always, after the Halloween ball
        Cast your costumes
        To the winds of fall.

Anonymous

It is a falling apart thing
That is dropping stuff on the thing
That is being written on
By the thing in my hand;
And the things are getting in the way of the thing.
It is a useful cool thing that is warming
In the other hand as my hand writes
With a thing on a thing
About a thing
That is a falling apart thing.

Anonymous

It's famous to me, but not to you.
It's close to me, but far to you.
I talk to it and think of it
But never had the guts to visit it.

Noise, violence, is where I liked to be,
But that's not the part that really makes me happy.
Noise and trains and cars that bang,
These were the things that I always had to see;
But it wasn't easy to have to leave these things
Because only I could see the good things that existed
In this beautiful city, where I'd like to be.

Veronica Wormley

JAMMED AND JELLIED

My mind is like downtown Boston at rush hour
Flooded with thoughts trying to cut each other off
To get home first.
It's clanking like gravel shaking in a tin can,
Like ten people trying to get through one door
Cluttered like a child's room,
Things thrown here and there
And nothing in its place;
Like trying to write this poem, all ideas jockeying
For position
Yet only a few are inked on paper.

Jane Plasse

Let's drench ourselves in fantasy
where moles go moo, and rocks can fly –
How high?
That doesn't really matter
for measurement is
endless here –
If moles go moo beneath the ground
the vibration of that very sound
would cause the rocks to fly
into space –
Let's race!

Let's drench ourselves in fantasy
where trees can walk
and sing to the sky,
Where birds can bark and fishes talk –
This must be my
destiny –

Let's drench ourselves in fantasy
where time goes through
and nothing dies.
If eyes are wise
but ears can't hear,
maybe there's no need to fear.

Let's drench ourselves in fantasy
where pamphlets yell with thirty feet
and fires turn purple on yellow glass,
Where cats can dance and doggies too
and chicken swim and fishes fly,

Where daisies don't get pulled apart
from "he loves me, he loves me not"
where rivers flow in spirals
and life goes ever on,
Where ears smell and fingers see –
What kind of person has this quality?
Surprise! It's me!

Let's drench ourselves in fantasy,
the pools of paint collecting
in the recesses of the ripplings
of heavy paper –
collecting places
for ourselves.

Let's drench ourselves in fantasy
where moles go moo and rocks can fly
and after all, do not forget
to say goodbye as they fly by,
Where fish will run, in a land of sun –
and there's lots of fun, under a blue blue sky,
Where mushrooms grow over ten feet tall,
and ants play dominoes in the fall,
Where trees can smile
and yellow is blue,
Where tables are used for walls
and all of us separated by them are not separated at all,
where dogs and cats work all day
and we play in the sun,

Where sheep can laugh
and man can cry.
This place is such an awesome
sight. It almost fills me
with great fright.
The flowers have faces.

Let's drench ourselves in fantasy
where stars peek out at
noontime
and people swim on land,
Where tumbleweeds paint desert scenes
and cactuses in a concert sing –
where children bring their dreams
to share with sand. and wind and air –
Where colors dance upon the eyelids
of all the hopefuls passing by,
where lilacs put on their shoes
of dew,
where caterpillars dance to a tune
or two
whistled by the wind, birds,
and a purple cock-a-poo,
and all is peaceful, loving.

A group poem from linea submitted by
members of an Elbanobscot/CETA mini course,
SENSITIVITY THROUGH POETRY WRITING,
October 11th, 1977

Light – dancing on the ceiling,
        Caught up on the fence out there,
        Its brilliance reflected so brightly on the icicle.
        It defies the eye to stare too long.
Now it's dripping down within
        The drops of water
        From the so long liquid sun.
        Where does it go when it's gone?
For it never really is.

Charlotte Cardeiro

Long ago, before memories,
God created spring
And everything went on from there.

The promise of a time of green,
Of feeling held closely
By a smiling sun.

If all there is around me
Can visibly turn
Into a thunderstorm of living,
Who am I to stay unmoved.

Not all is well
When spring sneaks up.
Its puppyish enthusiasm
Makes me mow
And mow some more!

Wim Jansen

MINDPLAY

Let's drench ourselves in fantasy
Where moles go moo, and haystacks see,
Where cats are green, and apples fly,
Where rocks do dance and textures cry,
Where clouds shake hands and names can roam
Inside my mind as in this poem.

Vincent Hayley

MUSIC, PROGRAM ME MY PAST

Tentative . . .
. . . strange . . . this
chamber of my self . . .
I . . . move . . . slowly . . .
toward its pulse . . .
. . . Now I can sit at the threshold . . .
Oh no! There's dust in the lyrics.
I can't hear . . . the music . . .
too obvious . . . too intense . . .
There's no logic to this . . .
bells peelaway . . . layer by layer . . .
I recede . . . back . . . and back . . .
an odyssey to inner space . . .
the labyrinth opens to atonal sounds . . .
now here, now there . . .

My ears are getting used to the dark.

*****

Again: I'm being pulled, led, taken, beyond

my boundaries . . . God help me!

1'm inside out!

* * * * *

A violin?
Asynchronous squeal! Return
to some familiar libretto.

Please.

Stop plunking along the old wild west.
For heaven's sake
Go west young man.

%#@***!!!

Whew! Thanks. I'd just completely
given up on civilization.

* * * * *

What . . . plunking along again?
What's a nice French horn like you doing
scraping along on silly frontiers like this?
Some melody . . . with no tune.
What now? Folding along across the Med club.
Accordions here too?
Pleats keep pizzas out of the west.
There's a quota on Italians here.
REWARD:
One marshal to maintain loud order.

*****

Plunking along again?
This time with violins.
This change of pace is too fast.
And here's . . . Tinker Bell, impersonated.
Please.
Return me to the other side of the rabbit hole.
                    Alice, can you hear me?
Dry your eyes and throw me an anchor.
I can't swim!

*****

Thank God. The finale. How alarming!
I can make myself wake up.
!!!!!

Rosie Rosenzweig

My O My
It's apple pie
Hockey, baseball
Spit in the eye
The End of freedom
Why? – Why?
Anesthetized - Socialized;
Priority diminished; choice denied.
Creativity, Individuality,
American fried.

Bananas and scallions in an apple orchard grow.
Brussel sprout and broccoli
Asparagrass to mow
Zuccini, oranges; fettish will be.
A sea of Ideas; it's dinner for me!

Barry Marchette

MYSTICAL MOTION

Music like the frame around a movie
Leads me slowly into a land so strange and familiar.
Look over there, my all-time-favorite cat
Still waiting for me to tickle her neck.
Listen, can't you hear
Her engine start within her kittenland of dreams,
And don't you see that stream dashing down,
And don't you feel the splashing of –
        music?
Now I walk, or is it dance,
And disappear,
Floating on sound;
Mystical motion knowing every move.

Wim Jansen

NATURE'S NEIGHBORS

The dandelions stretch
and look about.
A group of 15 kittens
prance through,
Happy in their field
of little suns
Who smile and sway
sharing their day.

Vincent Hayley

NEW BEDFORD GREEN

Clotheslines wave.
Leaves scamper in the morning wind.

Sunbathed branches dance.
Weeping willows grace the day
        with graceful sway.

The patriotic park bench waits for its public.
Golden grass reaches high.

A birdshadow climbs upon the roof
        as through the open park
A feathered friend glides
        atop a silky breeze.

The leaves of a windowbush gossip
        in the warmth of spring.

Vincent Hayley

NEW DAY

The squirrels, gray and sleepy eyed,
        Peek through the silver morning dew
                And stretch to greet the day.
A cool forest breeze wanders by.

Vincent Hayley

NEW WOODSTOCK

We seek success
Not knowing what it is.
We seek enthusiasm
Not knowing where it flames,
We seek tomorrow
Not thinking of today.
But growing we are,
And learning too –
Learning as we try to teach,
Learning about learning,
Learning about life.

Vincent Hayley

OCTOBERFROST

Geometries of satin sheen
Or clouds upon the lawn;
Calders on a field of green,
White shadows of the dawn.

Vincent Hayley

One of the greatest of sensual pleasures
    I've ever heard
Is feelings exchanged
    Without a word.

Charlotte Cardeiro

PAVILIONS OF THOUGHT

A kaleidoscope of images skipping
        in and out of view
A cacophony of ideas clamoring for birth,
        pushing, pulling at you, vying for position
Wave upon wave of emotion – fleeting
        yet not completely lost
Visions – far reaching and
        because they are yours
A canopy of dreams – spreading,
        building, enfolding the future
        and making it "now"
Remembrances – halting the wings of time
        so that "yesterday" becomes "today"

Sheila Scheufele

Peeking through my ears I see
Messages that delight me,
For the eyes are in harmony.

Charlotte Cardeiro

PLACES THAT I LOVE

I'd love to paint a fresco
        on these swirling plaster surfaces
        but I mustn't
The mood would be broken by
        the red orange and cadmium yellow
        I carry in my paint box

Marilyn Komins

PINEBRUSH

It is an unraveling log,
A feather,
A mole scampering through dry grass
A peppermint sky.
It is a porcupine of time,
A shale tree,
A flower of mud and wood,
A spider's land.

Vincent Hayley

RAINBOW TOWN

Red is green and blue is brown.
Paint the city yellow white, you're in town!

The steeples are gray, the fire trucks pink.
All flowers are violet, and orange is the sink –

Cars are purple with golden stars.
Trees are blue with yellow scars.

Roads are rosy – sometimes tan.
Now cool off – with a rainbow fan!

Corinne Nichols

REFLECTING ON MUSIC

Stillness – darkness –
Morning is entering the door;
The door of my mind opens,
The first rays of the sun peek in,
Then shadows appear to crowd out light.
Now the full blazing glory of light
Glowing, crowning glory of light;
Its sound is everywhere, echoing in my mind.

A desert scene – a new backdrop
For new sounds and sensations,
Wide spaces and endless horizon
Before me,
Weary, dry and never home.
I start my journey into the distance
Arriving at the place I have come away from;
My pace quickens as my heart hurries home.

Bobby Robinson

Ride the rubber raft
Through the rumbling roar
Of rolling rapids,
Rancorous and cantankerous
As they careen into the craft,
Rising and crashing
Roughed by the rambling rush
Of rampant rallies
Voracious in their repeated thrusts

Vincent Hayley

SEED

Small and smooth,
Deceptively dead,
Quiet and plain.
And yet it knows.
It has no doubts;
It knows.

Anonymous

SENSES

Once upon a fizelsnel
On the wide yellow wing of an imbuldeen
A tiny silfurdon laughed.
Nearby a radiant rendex arched
Into the deegsen of the holizop
And thought.

Vincent Hayley

SHADOWS

Where do shadows go at night?
Do they play tag on moonbeams?
Do they caress the velvet blue?
Do they talk of dreams?

Vincent Hayley

SHADOWS

The colors of life are black and white;
Shadows in the morning,
Shadows at night.

A pencil silhouette against the blue
Blends into a foggy view.
Does my shadow reveal an image
Or just a penciled personage –

One day the black will make its mark,
The white appears much sharper;
Until that time, the nights shall get no darker.

Shelba Levine

Shadows become different forms at night,
        unrestricted by the sun's light,
Brighter here, softer there,
        softer than a baby's hair.
The moon takes over where the sun leaves off.
        It must at times scoff
At the hard cold light of day.
        To hell with it – let's run through the moonshadows
        and play.

Charlotte Cardeiro

SINGLES BAR SCENE

Sugarloving candyrandies
Dandylioned suit and tie on
Snifferprattle diddle daddles
Sitting on a raised row of
Brassbarred red cushioned bar stools.

Marilyn Komins

Snow shadows slide
        across the satin soft snow
As the silver moon shines
        in silence
During the white night
        of lovers
Who stroll along the streets
        hands together
Sharing without a sound.

Vincent Hayley

SOJOURN

Time has been forgotten
And the forest is alive with rumors.

The large owl opens its mammoth wings
        and departs from a fallen trunk.
Stone walls wander through overgrown woodlands.
Flies buzz among leaves and shoreline stones.

A turquoise insect with long lace wings
        rests on a small rock.
The sun reflects a million spotlets
        on the gently oscillating pond.
A small clump of grass floats nearby
        with a few companion leaves.

The toppled birch reaches its many fingers
        into the water.
And the wispy sky shines a daylight blue.

Vincent Hayley

SONG OF THE SEA

The fire is a song I hear but cannot quite sing
        resting and rocking the warm air.
It enters the room from out of old volcanic rock
        now as dense as the dark past.
I've seen it in Hebraic cantellations
        in the rising and the falling
        of a scribe writing on parchment.
I know it like my own blood running unseen
        like an old wellspring
        a pillar –
It could erupt in clouds, tears
        and even death
To those who won't choose life
        and walk between the parting waves on the dry land
On this dancehall where the minstrels move
        with what we are,
        have been
        and always will be.

Rosie Rosenzweig

Sound of a daydream: Z Z Z
Sound of a seashore: C C C

To stop a horse you must say G.
To warm your innards, drink some T.

To circulate your thumbs, Twiddle D D.
To pollinate the plants, Bumble B B.

And if you like this poem
Just go Tee Hee Hee.

Corinne Nichols

SOUNDS AT NIGHT

The night owl hoots at night.
The bus's windshield wipers swish in the rain
Cars go quickly by my window, and
The seashore at the beach roars like a wild animal.

Karin Komins

SPRING

The crocus is the first I suspect to come up,
Then tulip and the sweet little yellow buttercup.

The colors so vivid – so purple and red,
The daffodils and irises in my flowerbed.

I look out each morning at the stone wall
And see a new bud – that's another inch tall.

Then two mornings later it's really in bloom;
I pick a bouquet and put it in my room.

Forsythia – lilacs – and dandelions too,
The grass – really green – and tree leaves so new.

This time of year I think is the best.
When summer arrives, spring takes a rest.

Corinne Nichols

Spring
Sun
Birch tree

Bird
Colorful feathers
Movements
Whistle
Song
Feathers
Twigs
Nest
Eggs

Wind   Sun   Rain

And MORE

Anonymous

SPRING 1978

I.
Why do you come upon me so quickly –
so suddenly full?
My heart still weathers the chill
Of this last cruel time.
I remember winter so well
That as I sit sunning with a warm breeze –

I shiver --

Backing off from the new turn.

II.
Can I believe the forsythia
After such a winter?
Is there perfume in the lilac still?
And the crabs -- one blooms and
The other still withholds --
And me, I curse the dandelions,
The weeds, the unkempt lawn
And freeze with the past.

III.
As the children set up for play
A seed stirs out of reluctance.
Summer promises and again
the world begins.

Rosie Rosenzweig

SPRING'S ENERGY

Spring comes popping out of the April sun
Comes riding in on the Southeast Breeze
Hopping along to the song of the tree toads
Dancing all over to the chirp of the birds
Dazzles our noses with *its* grand perfume
Ah! Enjoy!
It's almost June.

Charlotte Cardeiro

Spring, you are sunshine on my face,
A friendly cat nestling by as I write.
You are Christina's world and Gertrude Stein in one,
Hair blowing and thoughts flowing.
You are an apple tree dressed in white flower;
Bees visiting,
Cats watching ants at work.
You are a world outdoors.
You are life.

Vincent Hayley

STORM

The wind whips.
Waves reach high and hard and long.
Ocean homes move into the sea,
        piece by broken piece.
From knee-deep liquid streets
        people look with liquid eyes.

Farther inland, neighborhoods play.
Exiled cars are quiet, watching
Where streets have changed
        to fields of cheer.
Skiers slide and snowballs fly
        into the friendly afternoon.

Vincent Hayley

SUDBURY

The gray-green shaded waters of
        the quiet reservoir.
The moist sand plowed by swimmers' feet.
The welcome smell of a damp piece of wood,
        like a splashed pier.
Dead leaves, dangling like brown
        chandeliers in the wind.

Amid grass, some twigs repose.
Shore waters lap nearby.
A bird twitters.
A dragonfly almost walks on the pond.
The air is soft.

Vincent Hayley

SUNLIGHT

I am falling, gently falling
And to me the trees are calling
"Come and let us hold you in our arms."
To the tall ones, and the small ones
Winter numbed and huddled all ones
Rewarding faith and bringing nature's balm

Anonymous

SUNRISE

Slowly the city awakens
        from short hibernation.
Silence.
But here and there
        white boulders arch
        into the air.

Concrete rivers lie still.
Beneath a hill of white
        a nest door opens.
A tailed speck mews,
        delicately prancing
        into new mountains.
Eyes gaze upon the winter fluff.
Spots appear, growing into
        tunnels without ceilings,
        snowdoodles on their walls.

'Tis a yawn of dawn
three days long.

Vincent Hayley

SWIFTHOMAS

Swifthomas –
Bedraggled,
Beribboned,
Herringfish suit
Today's tye-dyed tie
Terryclothteakettle
Toothpasty cigar
Tremblebellied liar
Sets Sperry Handed snare

Marilyn Komins

TEAR DROPS IN THE SNOW

The icicle is a feat of gravity!

A delicate stylus, it melts into a self-
        made pit;
It clings with silky fingers to
        that mother of a roof.

This long thin fellow steals the rain
        in a capsule,
        crystallizes the snow
        in the capture of a watery well
        and sometimes curly,
        sometimes curtly,
Becomes a guillotine
that breaks the edge of spring.

Rosie Rosenzweig

THAT ISLAND IN TIME

Thursday is the first rose flush
Before the sunset that is Friday. We feel a hush
Surround us warm and soft as peach skins.
The candles soothe and fall around our evening prayers.
We break bread for a sky blue Sabbath at twilight
That cools the heated week behind.
Next – the day of rest, green and lush
Until we light the braided wicks again,
And smell the sharp spice of the new wind ahead.

Rosie Rosenzweig

The breeze upon the sail of my mind
Carries me far upon the day.
I feel a fresh relaxation.
It is a time when I can relax,
When I can enjoy,
Smelling the green of sweeping lawn
        Cascading.

Vincent Hayley

THE FEELING OF POETRY

Poetry is a feeling,
A feeling that's nice.
Everyone feels it
A lot more than twice.

It can be about anything:
A dog, an apple, a door,
An egg, a cat, or
Even a store.

Yes, poetry *is* a nice feeling!
I just felt it once more.

Cindy Smith

The fire in a fireplace –
Flames doing the dance of warmth and serenity,
    reaching upward in an attempt to make themselves
    felt,
Images ghostly and dreamy
    against a blackened backdrop;
Logs – some near death, some deceased
    crumbled into whitehot ashes,
    making way for new ones which give it life.

Sheila Scheufele

THE OUTSIDER

i want a front-seat ticket – the only one –
to the observation deck of your mindworks theater.
i want to watch the rotation of the
wheels and the pulleys that cause the
movement of the main-gear synthesis
that makes you what you are to the outside world.

Marilyn Komins

THE RIDDLE GIGGLE

At the market line the
Permanently curled man –
Chest and head –
Threw a canned line of jokes into my
Shopping cart.
My shopping cart giggled,
Throwing me off balance.

Marilyn Komins

The warm caress of sunshine upon my naked body
Is a butterfly fluttering above a golden quiet field
It is a mother cuddling her young.
It is a dancer leaping in delight,
A wind blowing gently on my face
As my sailboat glides silently
Over its wet and wonderful mirror.
It is a Monet countryside talking with me.
It is acceptance and joy.

Vincent Hayley

THE WIND

Kissing the earth
Ever so gently
With the sweet touch of my
Summer,
Howling and scowling over that
Same sweet breast in a
Twist of a mood
Quiet and serene, listless
Yet reposed – exhausted
Yet knowing that I am
Warming

Anonymous

THURSDAY

Morning sensuality of sun and air
        and self-caress.

Early, quiet Lake Dunmore.
My feet calmly swishing.

Young campers in towels.
Nude bathers
        in friendly conversation.

Twenty boys on a dock,
        their solid towels a palette
        of green, and pink,
        and beige, and blue, and aqua, and yellow.

A father and two youngsters.
Their silver rowboat gliding slow,
        fishing rod extended.

Canoeing the Middlebury with Jim and Sue.
My frustration while we journey
        to Jim's forgotten worms.
My anger
        as strenuously I oar,
        and Jim and Sue happily converse
        and Jim fishes.

Gondola pushes.
Shallow waters.
Portaging.
Pleasant pebbles as I step.

Paddling.
Shoreline trees silhouetted in the stream.
Naked dally.
Cool moving waters.

Distant thunder.
Darkening sky.
No lightning.

Tying the Great Canadian canoe
        atop the bronze Farrell Duster.

Light, long rainfall
        on the cottage and lake.
Chatting with Jim
        on the long screened porch.

Scanning Rivers Bend campgrounds
        for my weekend home.
Sightseeing by car.
Vermont landscapes
        sketched by Rembrandt.

Pinkish sunset.
Listening to unseen campers sing.

Sitting on the pier,
    my legs dangling in the water.
A distant soothing chant.

A nighttime dip.
The warm lake.
Enjoying my muscles
    as I breaststroke.

The night.

Vincent Hayley

Today, the most perfect day of spring.
I felt it on waking this morning
To the gentle chatter of birds.
The freshness of the day seeped
Into my room and beckoned me
To come and run away with it.
Today would be a day to cast everything
        aside
And run free and unhindered
        into the arms of spring,
Where everything is new and soft
And envelops you like little fingers
Massaging your soul.
Spring whispers softly, shouts sporadically
And grasps you by the hand,
Pulling you into its gentleness.
Sometimes I feel I could get lost in it
And never be afraid.

Sheila Scheufele

TO GOOSE CHICKS

The jolly twosome
Love to tease him
With his dancing smilemen
And roving beguilement.

To that Southie team
Who often beam,
Thanks. You add a shine
To friendship time.

Vincent Hayley

WALKING

Walking is like
A pattern on a piece of paper.
Endless.
After once
It can never be repeated.
Magic! Full of fun.

Cindy Smith

We are bound together,
You and me;
You a thread, and I a tree.

Together, somehow we were brought,
Your tender thread, a sturdy knot.
Who has this unnatural union wrought.

Ah, but though the knot is tight,
Resist any creeping fright.

Though firmly bound, we'll still be free,
You a thread, and I a tree.

Anonymous

WELLFLEET

I stand at the top of a 100 foot
sand dune on Cape Cod.
How strongly I feel the
presence of God,
His beautiful blue sky with clouds
softly floating by
The roaring powerful ocean –

I long to fly from the top
where I stand
Out over the ocean like the
gull above me.
Ah would that I were as free
as he.

Charlotte Cardeiro

What about us!
A pentameter of verse
A rhyme of writers
Of 2 + 4
2 boys, 4 girls
Some straight laced
And some in curls
Honing our words into a sharpened sense
A scribble of beauty
A touching of worlds

Charlotte Cardeiro, Vincent Hayley, Wim Jansen,
Corinne Nichols, Sheila Scheufele, and
Rosie Rosenzweig

What fun I'm having this sunny day
As I blow gently through the outstretched arms
Of m1ghty oaks
Which giggle as I tickle and pass.
What fun to swirl about the dusty streets
Of hometown folks,
Through big cities and little cities,
While children run through lawns and fields
To catch my kiss of summer.

Vincent Hayley

"What is intimacy?"
asked the priest about to marry.

I.
Only hermaphrodites are whole.
But that was long before Eden.
    The only thing that separates us now
    is one crisp bite of the apple . . .
        and that's long since fallen from our hands.

II.
So enter the craving,
    sometimes denied
        sometimes hidden
            but as present as the man himself.
Cities are built with its rationalizations:
    Sodom overflowed with its libations;
        that horrible magnificent sensation
            the craving . . .

III.
The work is to be whole with the One . . .
    Like living in a dark cave
        and playing with reflections
            We know not who we are
                or what we see
Until we speak . . . and . . . a whole life could spend itself
    in the first word.

IV.

The hardest is the breath that begins . . .
What words would follow . . . ?
"Me?" "You?"
That's for courting
. . . "We" is so far away
as far as Eden and the
apple . . .

Rosie Rosenzweig

WHITE FENCE

The pickets tall and crooked
Reaching out in space
Some close together – holding hands,
Ready to start the race –

The tips are stringy – small and plenty
Budded – and ready to flower.
The paint is peeling from the wind.
They form a modeled tower.

Corinne Nichols

WHITE WATER

Tumbling over stones,
Running past high banks
Turning as the bed turns
Slipping under bridges
Crashing over boulders
Ever onward
Cascading over cliffs
Leaping high into the air
Carrying with me
All that falls within
Rushing downward
Always forward
'Til my end is met

Anonymous

WHITE WIND

What a wind this day
Snowflakes hover,
Peek in my window,
And fly away.

Vincent Hayley

WINGED LOVE

What is this?
These docile birds sitting upon their perches
Don't they know they are king of the roost?
Wonder just why this is so?
Who the hell put the birds in limbo?
I think I know –
They are waiting for Esmerelda Doyle.
They cannot fly without her.

Charlotte Cardeiro

WINTERPLACE

Tonight
the sun has moved indoors –
and warms.

What a touch of pleasure
it has.

Framed in red brick
it lies in an orange ember bed
on a gray floor of transformed chemistry

I enjoy
and listen
and hear a mild whistle.

With a sound of flapping sails
a blond breeze reaches high
as webbed fingers of transparent yellow
wave between coats of cedar bark.

The thin carbon mist twists slightly
and floats skybound
while I sit and sense
heat
upon my cheek and arm and leg
this radiant winter day.

Vincent Hayley

WINTER VISIONS

Far from the flowers, this winter
I see the smell of purple –
the fascination of the bee
is mine

When those roses sense my nose,
my ears and eyes,
my me,
One with beauty.

Wim Jansen

Wood preserved by painted means;
Acrylic coating to redwood dreams,
Crumbled and rotten years gone by.
A home for waywood foragers;
Termites, fleas and gnats.

From forest primeval to picket fence
And then . . .
A resthome for foreign agents
And back home again.

Barry Marchette

You're like a group of pencils growing hair
So dark like graphite,
Your buds so alive
Waiting as newborn birds wait for food,
Surrounded by leaves and grass
Like a nest around your feet.

Tally Groves

Index by AUTHOR

Anonymous

Cardiero, Charlotte

Jansen, Wim

Komins, Karin

Komins, Marilyn

Levine, Shelba

Loftus, Mary

Index by PROCESS

DESCRIBING WITHOUT NAMING

FIRST LINES, To Start With

FLASH OF IMPRESSIONS

SOUNDS, Attending to

SPEAKING TO

SPECIAL MOMENTS, Written in the Present Tense

UNUSUAL PHRASING, Grouping with Words

Index by SUBJECT

CITIES AND SUBURBIAS

COUNTRY, WOODLANDS, AND WATERWAYS

ELEMENTS OF WEATHER

FANTASY

FIRES

INTIMACIES

NIGHTLIFE

OBSERVATIONS

PLACES

POETRY

SEASONS